Unlearning What Worked

Stories About Success, Stagnation, and Change

Matthew West-James

 West-Jamcs Press – Louisville, Kentucky, United States

Copyright © 2026 Matthew West-James

All rights reserved.

No part of this book may be reproduced or transmitted in any form or by any means, electronic or mechanical, including photocopying, recording, or any information storage and retrieval system, without prior written permission of the author, except for brief quotations used in reviews or scholarly discussion.

All photographs in this book are the property of the author unless otherwise noted.

Any trademarks, service marks, product names, or logos appearing in this book are the property of their respective owners. Their use is for identification purposes only and does not imply endorsement.

Published by West-James Press
Louisville, Kentucky, United States

Library of Congress Control Number: 2026901646
ISBN: 979-8-9946232-1-3

First edition

DEDICATION

For my children,
Michael, Jacob, and Cassandra.

For my wife,
Caryl "Michelle" West-James

For my parents,
Michael "Brian" James and Veronica James

For Jeffrey Leftwich
And Kevin Holzknecht,

The people who believed in me when the path forward was unclear.

CONTENTS

1	Introduction to the Reader	1
2	Crossing My Rubicon	5
3	Growth Runs Both Ways	11
4	The Cost of Invisibility	17
5	Ask Forgiveness, Not Permission	21
6	Whisper Campaigns	27
7	Ethical Escalations	31
8	Nice Guy Finishes Last	37
9	SPLAT Award	41
10	Bad Decision vs No Decision	47
11	Grace and Forgiveness	53
12	Getting Help for the Wrong Reason	59
13	The Costs of Change	65
14	Closing	71

"The unexamined life is not worth living."

—Socrates

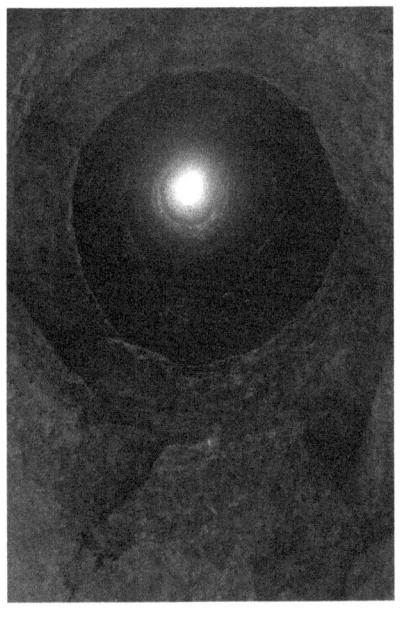

1 INTRODUCTION TO THE READER

This book is about unlearning what worked before.

I set out to write this as a collection of stories from my life and career, not because my story is extraordinary, but because it is ordinary in ways that matter. These stories span different roles I have held and identities I have lived as a disaster response volunteer, a soldier, an IT professional, a father, and, most importantly, as a human being trying to make sense of things as they unfold.

Are these stories unique? Not really. That is the point. The experiences and themes they touch on are ones most people will recognize. Almost every reader will find something here that sparks a moment of recognition. A quiet, "yeah, that feels familiar." A realization that they are not alone in thinking or feeling the way they do.

This book is not meant to be read like a manual. With the exception of this introduction and the closing, most chapters stand on their own. The order exists because books have to have an order, not because these stories build toward a single conclusion. If something catches your attention, start there. If a chapter does not resonate, skip it. Think of this less as a linear argument and more as a collection you can move through in whatever way makes sense to you.

Over time, I have learned a simple but uncomfortable truth: just because something works does not mean it is the best tool for the job.

Sometimes it only works because the context has not changed yet. Other times, it works right up until it does not.

As an IT professional, I argue about this constantly. There is always a new technology, a new framework, a new solution that promises to fix everything. Right now, that solution is artificial intelligence, more precisely large language models, imperfect but evolving. To be clear, AI is not a fad in the sense that it will disappear. It is powerful, transformative, and here to stay. But believing any single tool can solve every problem is how we stop thinking critically. Tools are only effective when they are used with intention, context, and humility.

The same mistake applies outside of technology. In life, we cling to strategies that once kept us safe, successful, or accepted. We mistake familiarity for correctness. We mistake survival for growth. We keep using the same tools because they worked once, even when they quietly begin to cost us more than they give back.

From the outside, my life looks pretty good. I am a senior individual contributor in my field. I own my home. I have two cars and three beautiful children. None of that is false. And yet, for a long time, my career felt stalled. Not because things were going badly, but because I crave new challenges and new things to fix. I do not like the feeling of treading water. What I eventually realized is that no career offers constant growth, at least not for most people. What had changed was not my situation, but what I was seeking. I was no longer chasing money so much as meaning.

One of my mistakes along the way was internalizing work as my primary measure of value. I treated my career as proof of worth, both to myself and to the world. Over time, I had to confront the reality that work is just work. A bad career, or even a stalled one, does not make a person undeserving of notice. Systems, especially large ones, are often indifferent. Extra effort may be rewarded eventually, but there is no guarantee. Understanding that was uncomfortable, but necessary.

For a long time, survival shaped my habits. Survival is about getting from one point to another without regard for quality. Growth is different. Growth cares about quality, pacing, and sustainability. The problem is that survival habits have a way of becoming permanent unless we stop to examine them. That is something I have struggled with. I believe I have moved from survival toward growth, but it required change, and change required letting go of strategies that once kept me afloat.

That is what I mean by unlearning.

The reader's work, if there is any, is simply to look at the tools that have served them well and ask whether those tools still do. Some will. Some may not. One small example for me was reconsidering the cultural artifact of the two-week notice. After an honest review, I chose to keep it, not because I believe employers inherently deserve it, but because good bosses often do. That decision may change in the future. The point is not what you keep or discard, but that you pause long enough to decide.

This book is a reflection on that process. Not a guide. Not a prescription. Just an honest accounting of moments where what once worked had to be questioned, softened, or abandoned entirely.

Some of these stories are polished. Others are not. Some are strong. Some are weaker. That is intentional. Growth is rarely linear, and clarity often comes after the fact. This is not a manifesto. It is a record of learning in progress.

If you take anything from these pages, I hope it is this: you are allowed to outgrow the tools that once helped you survive. You are allowed to set them down, even if they once served you well. And you are allowed to pick up new ones, even if they feel unfamiliar at first.

"If you are going through hell, keep going."

—Winston Churchill

2 CROSSING MY RUBICON

There was a point in my career where I felt stuck, not lost exactly, but pinned in place.

I had recently been hired into my first healthcare IT role. I was eager, motivated, and very deliberately chasing what felt like the holy grail at the time: becoming a network engineer. On paper, I was doing everything right. I already had my bachelor's degree. I was actively working on a master's degree. I had certifications coming out of my ears, Cisco, VMware, Juniper, and more. Yet no matter how hard I pushed, nothing seemed to move.

I kept telling myself to just keep doing good work, that eventually it would pay off. But I was also painfully aware that promotions often depend on timing, politics, and forces entirely outside your control. I wanted something I could influence directly. Something that would move the needle without requiring someone else's permission.

That hesitation about tying my identity too tightly to an institution wasn't new.

Even in college, I refused to buy a T-shirt with the school's logo on it. Not because I disliked the school, but because I was afraid of what it would mean if I failed. I didn't want a physical reminder of something I hadn't yet earned. I bought my first college shirt at Western Kentucky University only after I decided I was going to finish my degree. Only then did it feel safe to let the university's identity overlap with my own.

That pattern mattered, even if I didn't fully recognize it at the time.

So, like many people in IT, I found myself scrolling through Reddit.

I came across a post from someone else in tech who was volunteering their skills to nonprofits. The idea clicked immediately, not because of altruism, but because of résumé math. Volunteer experience. Leadership exposure. Something different. That same day, I signed up for three organizations. One of them was Team Rubicon.

Team Rubicon is a veteran-led disaster response organization that takes much of what works in the military, structure, mission focus, and shared purpose, and repurposes it for humanitarian work. There are no salutes and no rank that really matters. There is simply a job that needs to be done and people willing to do it. At the time, that familiarity appealed to me more as an idea than as a calling.

To be honest, my intentions were not noble. I was not trying to help people. I was trying to help myself. I wanted a stronger résumé and a clearer path forward in a career that felt stalled.

What truly hooked me was the idea of a large international deployment, one that felt urgent, visible, and deeply consequential as the impacts of a disaster dominated the news and social media.

When Hurricane Dorian hit the Bahamas, Team Rubicon's response filled my inbox. That mission appealed to an idealized version of myself, the guy who shows up, makes a difference, and leads without hesitation. A selfless, fearless leader. That was who I wanted to be seen as, and maybe who I wanted to believe I already was.

The harder truth is that even if I had gone, I wasn't actually willing to take the risks required to be that person. I wanted the identity more than I was ready to accept the cost.

I completed the background checks, the online classes, and everything required to be deployable. I wanted to go. I wasn't selected, which in retrospect made complete sense. You don't send someone brand new into another country to work in a disaster zone. At the time, it was disappointing. Later, it felt appropriate.

After that, the momentum faded. Life continued. Work stayed the same. Team Rubicon receded into the background. If I'm honest, smaller and more local disasters didn't interest me much then. They didn't feel significant enough to justify the disruption.

Then COVID-19 hit.

COVID-19 was a major crisis, and I wanted to help. As the pandemic unfolded, volunteers became harder to find, travel became restricted, and yet disasters didn't stop happening. Tornadoes still hit. Floods still came. Natural disasters don't take a break during other disasters, even when those disasters are political or biological.

With fewer people able or willing to respond, Team Rubicon became one of the few places where I could help without needing permission. I wasn't inserting myself or trying to manufacture relevance. I was actively being asked.

When a tornado hit Arkansas, I signed up.

I talked to my boss and explained that I felt it was important, particularly during the pandemic, to help people. I packed my car and drove nearly the maximum distance Team Rubicon allowed, close to 600 miles. I arrived ready to contribute whatever skills I had.

And that's when I learned a humbling lesson.

They didn't need my IT skills at all.

What they needed was swamping.

Swamping is simple and brutal work. Someone with a chainsaw goes ahead, cutting fallen trees into manageable sections. My job was to drag those sections, load them onto a sled, and haul them to the curb. Over and over again. It was exhausting, dirty, physically demanding work, the kind you feel in your hands, your back, your legs, and your lungs.

And somehow, it was exactly what I needed.

For the first time in a long time, I felt useful in a way that had nothing to do with titles, credentials, or career ladders. There was a clarity to the work. You showed up. You did the job. You helped someone reclaim a small piece of their life after chaos had taken it.

Being in that pseudo-military environment was unexpectedly cathartic. I had been out of the Army long enough to forget how much I missed the structure, the shared mission, and the quiet understanding that everyone was there for something bigger than themselves. I felt like I belonged again. I felt purpose.

Here's the part that still matters most to me. I didn't join Team Rubicon to be a good person. I joined for selfish reasons. But somewhere between the chainsaws, the sweat, and the exhaustion, something shifted.

That experience became a pivot point in my life.

Within Team Rubicon, there is an unspoken cultural tradition. Some people choose to mark their commitment the same way service members have for generations, by carrying the symbol on their body. It's not required. It's not encouraged. But it's understood. It's less about the organization itself and more about acknowledging that something inside you changed.

Getting the tattoo was a personal point of no return for me.

Given my history, that mattered more than it might for someone else. I had spent years avoiding permanent alignment with institutions out of fear that I might fail them or myself. Even a college T-shirt had once felt like too much commitment. A tattoo was different. It was permanent enough that I couldn't easily separate myself from it.

Yes, tattoos can technically be removed, but anyone who says that misses the point. Even if the ink were gone, the choice would not be. I didn't get it on a whim. I got it because I wanted my outside to display the internal alignment I had made, to commit to a cause in a way I couldn't quietly walk away from.

The tattoo wasn't about Team Rubicon defining me forever. It was about me crossing a line I didn't intend to cross back over. It was my Rubicon.

While Team Rubicon isn't as central in my life as it once was, that moment still shapes me. It was where I finally internalized a lesson, we're taught our entire lives but rarely feel in our bones. One person can't change the world, but one person can absolutely change the world for someone.

I still chase that feeling.

Not the adrenaline. Not the recognition. But the quiet certainty that, in that moment, what I did mattered to someone else.

And that has made all the difference.

"We don't receive wisdom; we must discover it for ourselves after a journey that no one can take for us."

— Marcel Proust

3 GROWTH RUNS BOTH WAYS

Throughout my life, I wanted to be good at things, or at least not look foolish in front of other people. That desire, I later learned, was tied closely to social anxiety, but at the time I just knew it limited me. I learned quickly that being different was costly.

As a small child, well before I ever started school, I decided I wanted to study insects. When adults asked what I wanted to be when I grew up, I proudly told them I wanted to be an entomologist. They would smile, then look at my parents and ask, "Is that a real thing?" My parents would explain what it was.

I had a strong drive to be curious, creative, and different. But once I got to school, that didn't work out very well.

I was bullied. Consistently. Through grade school, high school, and even a little in the military. Over time, I learned a lesson that felt necessary for survival: it was safer to be invisible. Stay inside the lines. Don't stand out.

As a father, I worried I might pass that lesson on to my children. That I would unintentionally teach them to shrink themselves the way I had learned to do.

To my surprise, they didn't internalize it.

My children pursue things with a willingness I never had. One of my sons does archery. I never really did school sports. I still remember Little League, once we switched from pitching machines to real pitchers. Some pitchers intentionally hit me with the ball. It happened too often to be accidental. I'd cry. I'd take the walk. I quickly decided I wasn't good at baseball, and I absorbed another rule: if you're not good at something, don't put yourself out there.

My son didn't learn that rule. He took the risk anyway. He does archery because he wants to, not because he's chasing being the best.

My other son does choir. Singing was something I loved as a kid, especially in groups, where mistakes disappeared into the sound around you. When it became uncool to sing, I tried going against the grain for a while. But once you're one of only a few voices, every imperfection stands out. I was bullied for it. I learned the lesson and moved on.

My daughter loves art. I stopped drawing years ago because I didn't think I was "good enough." Only recently have I tried again. I don't expect my work to end up in a museum, but I enjoy the process, and I do think I have creative things to say.

The moment it crystallized for me that my children were learning something different than I had was when my son, then an early teenager, told me what he wanted to do for Halloween.

He wanted to wear a rainbow-themed costume to support gay rights.

I don't know if my son is gay, and it doesn't matter. My concern wasn't about that. My concern was about him being bullied or even something worse. About him being made to feel lesser. That fear lives deep in me.

I also worried, quietly, about whether turning something meaningful into a Halloween costume might be taken the wrong way. Whether people would see it as trivializing or mocking the very thing he was trying to support. That concern came from the same place as the rest of my hesitation: a fear of unintended harm.

And I worried about something else, too. This was a polarizing issue.

I knew how children could react, but I also knew how adults sometimes do. Classmates were one thing. The idea that a teacher or staff member might single him out, even subtly, for holding a visible position on a controversial topic unsettled me just as much.

All of that fear was mine.

None of it was his.

So I talked to him. I told him I loved the idea, but that it might make other people angry. My wife, his stepmother, and I both shared our concerns with him openly. We weren't trying to shut him down, only to help him think through how his message might be received.

He looked at me and said, "That's their problem, not mine."

I remember asking him what he meant.

He said, "I have to do what I think is right."

It was more important to him, he explained, to be true to himself and his values than to worry about how other people might react.

We talked it through together and reached a compromise. If he wanted to make a statement, he could choose a well-known gay rights icon and dress as them instead. He agreed easily, not because his conviction wavered, but because he was willing to engage in the discussion.

In the end, he abandoned the idea altogether.

Not because he was worried about optics. Not because he had backed away from his beliefs. He abandoned it for a far more ordinary reason: he decided it was boring. Too common. Halloween, in his mind, was still about dressing up, and he chose to go as a demon instead.

What struck me wasn't the costume he ultimately wore. It was the reasoning behind it.

He hadn't stopped caring about gay rights. He simply didn't feel the need to center them in that moment. Support for people different from himself was already normalized for him. It wasn't a statement he felt compelled to make. It was a given.

In some ways, that showed something even better than defiance.

It's humbling how much we learn from our children.

Even as a middle-aged parent, my son taught me something I never fully learned when I was younger: when it comes to values, when it comes to what actually matters, you don't always have to announce them loudly. Sometimes the truest measure is how naturally they are lived.

I admire his bravery and his certainty. Some of that will soften with age, with experience, with reality. But that core value, that quiet confidence in who he is and what he believes, I don't think that will ever go away.

And knowing that I helped create that, that my parenting played a role in that foundation, is probably one of the greatest achievements of my life.

"If you are silent about your pain, they'll kill you and say you enjoyed it."
— Zora Neale Hurston

4 THE COST OF INVISIBILITY

There's a lesson I learned in the military that stayed with me far longer than it should have.

I was lower enlisted. An E-4. Part of what we jokingly called the "sham shield mafia." The unspoken rule was simple: never volunteer for anything unless you knew exactly what it involved, and even then, your real goal was to be just invisible enough not to be noticed when unpleasant work appeared.

It was a survival strategy. And it worked.

Like many things that kept me safe early in life, it quietly followed me forward, long after the environment that created it was gone.

Somewhere along the way, though, I stopped recognizing it as a tactic and started carrying it as a worldview. Being invisible felt safer. Not just in the military, but in my career, my leadership, and my sense of self.

That belief followed me into my volunteer work with Team Rubicon.

I became active during the COVID-19 pandemic, driven by the need to help and to be useful. I took every training course I could, including one designed to prepare volunteers to handle logistics for small, local disaster responses. On paper, I was qualified. In practice, I had never actually done the job.

During a deployment in Louisiana, I was told they needed someone to take on that logistics role. I hesitated. I explained that while I had the training, I lacked real experience, and someone else might be better suited. The incident commander waved that concern away. I would be supported, he said. I would learn as I went.

And I did. But logistics is not something you ever fully learn in a classroom. It's too big, too interconnected, too dependent on judgment and delegation.

That reality hit me hard during the tornado response in Mayfield, Kentucky.

What was expected to be a small operation grew rapidly. Before I fully processed what was happening, I found myself responsible for logistics at a national scale disaster response. People. Supplies. Vehicles. Food. Shelter. Showers. Every problem eventually landed on my desk.

I was terrified of failing publicly.

So I reverted to what had always kept me safe. I made myself invisible by making myself indispensable. I took on everything. I delegated only when explicitly required to. When I was told I had to assign someone to handle food operations, I did so reluctantly.

That role, like many in logistics, is critical and almost entirely unseen. If it's done well, no one notices. If it's done poorly, everything falls apart.

For everything else, I tried to carry it alone.

The deployment lasted a week, maybe two. I genuinely don't remember. I slept an average of two hours a night. I was constantly solving problems. Buying supplies. Fueling vehicles. Figuring out how to keep a shower trailer from freezing overnight so volunteers could bathe. Every issue came to me because I had positioned myself as the center of the system.

I told myself I was being responsible.

In reality, I was becoming the single point of failure.

Later deployments forced me to confront that truth. Slowly, uncomfortably, I learned how to delegate. How to trust. And more importantly, I learned that trust in leadership cannot be one-directional.

For a long time in my career, I believed people didn't trust me. What I eventually realized was harder to accept: I wasn't trusting them either.

Delegation isn't abdication. It's not random assignment or wishful thinking. It's paying attention. Seeing people clearly. Developing them. On later operations, I learned to match people to roles based on their strengths. Someone skilled in the field might thrive managing equipment and supplies. Someone else might be better suited to coordination or planning.

When I trusted people with responsibility, they grew into it. When I stopped trying to be invisible, stopped trying to carry everything myself, the operation became stronger.

Invisibility had once kept me safe. But leadership required something different.

One person cannot do it all. Span of control matters. Everything collapses when you make yourself the only load-bearing wall.

That lesson was hard-earned. I'm still learning it. But it marked a shift for me, from surviving quietly to leading visibly, and from hiding behind competence to building trust that flows both ways.

"Do what you can, with what you have, where you are."

— Theodore Roosevelt

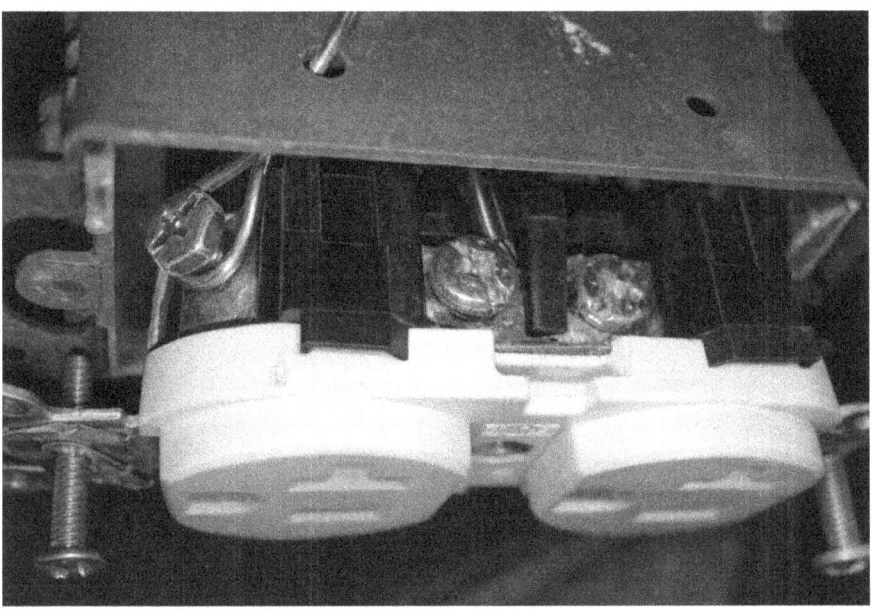

5 ASK FORGIVENESS, NOT PERMISSION

"It's better to ask forgiveness than permission."

That's one of those lessons I picked up in the military. Not an official rule, not something written down, but something you absorb, especially when you never move beyond lower enlisted. You learn to operate in the margins. To act first, explain later.

What I didn't understand yet was that initiative is judged less by intent and more by how far its impact reaches.

I carried that lesson with me into my healthcare IT career.

After moving from NOC technician to network engineer, my role changed in one key way: I joined the on-call rotation. And at first, on call was brutal. Middle-of-the-night interruptions for things that were often trivial. Printer reservations. Minor alerts. Things that absolutely did not require waking someone up at 2 or 3 a.m.

So I took the initiative.

I started writing procedures, tightening rules, and tuning monitoring for the Network Operations Center, which was staffed 24/7 but still relatively new and underutilized. Over time, those changes worked. On-call went from a constant disruption to something I barely noticed. Maybe one call a week. Sometimes none at all.

That initiative was tolerated and accepted because it stayed within my lane. It improved outcomes without changing structures. It didn't affect budgets, titles, or anyone else's standing. It solved a problem without creating new ones.

That success made me ambitious.

I decided that being a network engineer wasn't enough anymore. I wanted to manage the NOC. I went to my manager and told him directly that I wanted to take management control of the group. I believed the lack of centralized oversight was holding it back, and I could take on that responsibility and make his job easier.

He didn't shut me down. In fact, he told me it was an admirable goal. But he also told me the truth: budget and politics didn't allow for a new manager position.

I heard that as, "Wait."

I wasn't happy with waiting.

Around that time, we had moved into a new building. The NOC was physically separate from the rest of the office space, and there was a dedicated office designed for a NOC manager. At the moment, it was being used mostly for storage.

And that's where I made a decision.

Instead of asking permission, I would ask for forgiveness. I cleared the storage out, moved my desk and laptop in, hooked up a phone, and started working from that office. Almost immediately, something interesting happened. People saw me in the space. They assumed authority. They asked questions. I answered them or directed them to the right teams.

By taking the office, I wasn't just claiming space. I was unintentionally signaling authority I hadn't been given.

For about 24 hours, it felt like the experiment worked.

Then I got the email.

My manager told me it was fine for a short-term project, but that office was not my space and I needed to move out of the office.

There's an important piece of context here. At the same time, I was struggling in my assigned workspace due to PTSD. Having my back to a main walkway was triggering. I startled easily. I was constantly on edge. That office felt safer, but safety alone didn't justify the way I went about it.

So I replied to the email and acknowledged that I would move. I explained why I had taken the office, focusing on the PTSD side of the choice, and admitted that I probably should have gone to HR for a reasonable accommodation instead of acting unilaterally.

That email triggered a phone call.

My manager didn't yell, but I knew him well enough to know he was furious. What I didn't know at the time was that he had recently been through an HR complaint and was extremely sensitive to anything involving accommodations or HR processes.

I had to explain my reactions to sudden unexpected changes, even as small as someone walking to the restroom. I reminded him that he knew about my PTSD. He had seen it firsthand, years earlier, when I worked in data centers and would jump or shout if someone appeared unexpectedly behind me.

He acknowledged that he did know.

To his credit, he acted. He arranged for me to move to a different cubicle, one that wasn't in a main walkway, and the immediate issue was mitigated.

Looking back, the experience was both good and bad.

The real problem wasn't initiative itself. It was scale.

When my initiative improved the NOC without affecting anyone else, it was welcome. When it began to affect people outside our management silo, even if only through optics, it became a problem. I moved from improving a system to reshaping perception without understanding the broader context.

The organization was downsizing office space at the time. People who once had offices were being moved into cubicles. It would never have been acceptable for an individual contributor to occupy a dedicated office while managers and other senior employees lost theirs.

I didn't see that. I should have.

The lesson wasn't that initiative is dangerous. It's that initiative without context is.

Acting boldly inside a system you understand can be leadership. Acting boldly without understanding how far the ripples travel is just motion.

That day, I learned the difference.

"A lie can travel halfway around the world while the truth is still putting on its shoes."

— Mark Twain

6 WHISPER CAMPAIGNS

Whispers and rumors can be an effective way to get information.

They can also be an effective way to give information. The danger is that informal communication rarely lands exactly where you intend it to. Sometimes the knives end up in your own back. Sometimes these knives can end up in the backs of the people you trust most and who are actively trying to support you.

Throughout my childhood, my time in the military, college, and my early career, I learned to listen. I paid attention to what people said when they thought no one important was listening. By doing that, I often learned things I was not technically supposed to know, but that helped me understand what was really happening around me.

When I started a new job at a small rural cable company, I believed I was upgrading my career in a meaningful way. I moved from a NOC technician role into a Director of Information Technology title. On paper, I received a ten-thousand-dollar raise, access to a company vehicle, and what looked like a significant step forward.

As often happens in very small organizations, the title was inflated. While my salary increased on paper, the reality was different. At my previous employer, health insurance was heavily subsidized. At this new company, the contribution was minimal. The result was that despite the apparent raise, my actual take-home pay was lower than before at the regional cable company.

My job was based out of a somewhat remote rural office that also functioned as a self-storage facility. I worked primarily alongside a customer service agent at the front desk and a field technician who handled installations and repairs. It did not take long for me to realize that information flowed freely upward from that office, whether intentionally or not.

I raised the compensation issue directly with my supervisor, who held the equally impressive title of Vice President of Operations. I explained more than once that I had effectively taken a pay cut and that I needed to be able to support my family.

Then I had what I thought was a clever strategic idea.

I began openly complaining about being underpaid, sometimes within earshot of the customer service agent and sometimes directly to them. I talked about how much I liked the job but could make more elsewhere, and how my compensation didn't align with my title or responsibilities. Predictably, that information traveled upward. Eventually, my supervisor pulled me aside and told me, very directly, to knock it off.

At the time, I thought I had made a master stroke. The issue had visibility. Conversations followed. We ultimately arrived at a creative solution that increased the company's health insurance contribution, raising my effective take-home pay without requiring a long-term salary commitment from the business. From a tactical perspective, it worked.

That success almost convinced me it was the right approach.

What I failed to understand was the collateral damage. The message that reached ownership was not simply that I was struggling financially. It was that I believed I was more important than the role. That I might be difficult to manage. That perhaps the company should consider changing my position or removing me altogether.

More importantly, it created problems for my supervisor. He believed my results justified some of my behavior and was actively trying to protect me. My indirect communication made that harder. I had not thought through the second-order effects of using informal channels as leverage.

Not long after my supervisor left the organization for another role, I was laid off. While there were multiple factors involved, I believe this episode played a role. My former supervisor believed I was worth the effort. Ownership and other leadership did not believe they could support the growth I wanted or the way I went about pursuing it. Quite frankly, I had not communicated my needs in an effective or professional manner.

Years later, after both of us had moved on, I spoke with my former supervisor about it. I explained what I had done and why I had done it. His response was blunt, honest and direct.

"That was really stupid. You should not have done that."

He was right.

There is value in informal communication. Listening to rumors and whispers can be an effective way to take the pulse of an organization, and it is something I still do. Listening, however, is not the same thing as communicating. My mistake was trying to turn observation into a strategy for influence.

Since then, I have been far more deliberate about how I communicate concerns, expectations, and even aspirations. Informal networks are powerful, but they are not neutral, and they always have an audience. Listening remains a valuable tool. Using whispers as leverage was not. In this case, the tactic worked, but it quietly undermined trust, damaged relationships, and taught me a lesson that stayed with me far longer than the raise ever did.

"Neutrality helps the oppressor, never the victim."

— Elie Wiesel

7 ETHICAL ESCALATIONS

Through my experiences in the military, I came to deeply understand the value of chain of command and the importance of addressing issues at the lowest appropriate level. In the Army, that structure was explicit. You had a squad, then a platoon, then a company. If you had a problem, you brought it to your squad leader. If it couldn't be resolved, you asked permission to escalate it to the next level. As a lower-enlisted soldier, I almost never operated beyond the company level, but the lesson was clear: respect the hierarchy, work within it, and escalate only when necessary.

When I transitioned into my professional career after the military and college, I carried that mindset with me.

My first professional job was at a cable company, where I was hired as a contract-to-hire employee. For the first six months, I technically worked for another company and received no benefits, including health insurance. That mattered deeply to me. I wanted to start a family, but I knew I couldn't responsibly do that without medical coverage. Converting to full-time employment wasn't just about career advancement. It was about stability and responsibility.

As the six-month mark passed, I began asking questions. I went to my supervisor to ask when I could expect to become a full-time employee. He told me I needed to speak with my manager. So I did.

That process was not easy. I worked third shift, while most management worked standard daytime hours, which meant staying late after long nights just to attend meetings. During that time, I did receive raises. Based on informal chatter, I was among the lowest-paid technicians, and my manager did what he could within his authority. More than once, he would approve a raise and then ask why I was still coming to his office.

The answer was simple: raises did not solve the problem I was trying to address. I wanted to start a family, and I did not believe it was responsible to do so without health insurance. As it turned out, that concern was well-founded. When my first child arrived, he brought his twin with him.

Each conversation ultimately ended the same way. My manager told me my performance was strong, but the decision to convert me to full-time employment wasn't his to make. It belonged to the director.

At first, I accepted that explanation. Over time, however, it became clear that "just wait" was the only answer I was going to get. Eventually, I reached a point where I felt I had exhausted every appropriate level in the hierarchy. I had followed the chain. I had done what I was taught to do.

Deciding to email the director directly was not easy. My concern wasn't being told no. It was the fear of retaliation from my manager, the fear of being labeled difficult, or worse, of being seen as entitled. In hierarchical environments, those labels can quietly follow you. Still, I felt that remaining silent carried its own risks.

I emailed the director and asked if I could meet with him when he arrived at the office that morning. He agreed.

So I waited.

I was asked not to wait in the NOC itself, because it gave the impression that I was supposed to be working but wasn't doing my job. There were no chairs outside the offices, nowhere to sit and disappear. Instead, I leaned against the wall near the director's office, wandered the hallway, or refilled my coffee cup in the breakroom. I tried to look occupied without looking defiant.

It was almost painful.

I was exhausted and ready to go home and get some sleep, but I stayed. As the hours passed, the confidence I had felt earlier began to erode. Standing there, half-invisible and fully exposed, I started replaying every possible outcome in my head. Maybe this was a mistake. Maybe I had misread the situation. Maybe I had pushed too far and would pay for it later.

Most of the waiting happened internally. I weighed the cost of staying against the cost of walking away. I asked myself whether this effort was worth it, whether advocating for myself in this way was the right move, or whether silence would have been safer. There was no certainty, only the slow passing of time and the growing awareness that whatever happened next, I had already crossed a line I couldn't uncross.

So I stayed.

My shift ended, and instead of going home to sleep, I stayed at the office. A few hours later, my manager pulled me aside. He was visibly angry and made it clear he was unhappy with my decision. He told me the meeting wouldn't change anything and that I needed to accept the process and wait.

There was more behind his reaction than simple frustration. My manager was also a recent combat veteran. In fact, I had been slated to join his reserve unit after completing my job classification training, but due to my specific classification, I was reassigned elsewhere. From his perspective, I had violated a deeply ingrained military rule: you do not escalate past a leader without explicit permission. What I saw as appropriate escalation likely looked to him like a breach of discipline.

Respectfully, I told him I was going to stay and speak with the director.

The director was delayed that morning due to what he later described only as an emergency. I never knew whether it was work-related, family-related, or personal, but the delay meant hours more waiting and plenty of time to reconsider whether I had made a mistake. Eventually, he arrived, and we sat down together.

I explained why becoming a full-time employee mattered to me, how important stability and benefits were, and how committed I was to growing with the company. I also told him plainly that if there were any performance issues or areas where I needed to improve, I wanted to know.

His response and demeanor surprised me. This was my boss' boss' boss, and I had expected formality and distance. Instead, he was kind, calm, and effortlessly charismatic. We talked at length about my goals and why they mattered to me. He offered guidance on how to position myself better within the organization and explained the kinds of things leadership paid attention to.

I pressed for specifics. I wanted clear, actionable direction. Should I pursue a particular vendor certification? Would earning one credential over another materially change my prospects? He told me those things were not bad ideas, but they were unlikely to move the needle in the way I was hoping. What mattered more, he said, was continuing to do the quality of work I was already doing and allowing time for that reputation to compound.

He made it clear there were no concerns with my performance. It wasn't just good, it was excellent. There was nothing specific I needed to fix. I simply needed to be patient.

I left that meeting exhausted and uncertain, but at peace with the fact that I had advocated for myself. I went home to get a few hours of sleep before returning for my next third-shift rotation.

A few hours later, I received a call.

By that point, I had gone home and collapsed into sleep almost immediately. When my phone rang, it pulled me out of a deep, disorienting sleep. For a moment, I wasn't even sure where I was, let alone what was happening. I answered groggily, trying to piece together reality as I listened.

On the line were both my manager and the director. They told me that while the meeting I had requested had "no impact whatsoever," the decision had been made to convert me to a full-time employee. The timing was, they said, purely coincidental.

When the call ended, I wasn't entirely sure it had actually happened. It wasn't until I returned to work the next day and saw the emails confirming it that the moment fully settled into reality.

In hindsight, I know that outcome was not guaranteed. Even strong performance and persistence can be blocked by business realities. Timing, budgets, and organizational needs can override individual merit. But I also know my meeting mattered. It made me visible. It put a real person behind the request.

More importantly, it changed my relationship with the director. After that, he became someone I could regularly go to for professional guidance. Those conversations led to being pulled into projects and given broader exposure. When he later chose to leave for a smaller rural cable company, he invited me to come with him. That single meeting became the foundation of a mentorship that followed me across multiple employers and shaped the trajectory of my career.

At the time, emailing him felt like a foolhardy risk. Looking back, it was one of the best decisions I ever made.

What I learned from that experience is that raw ability by itself is rarely enough. Skills matter, effort matters, and performance matters. But growth happens when trust is built. Careers move forward not just because of what you can do, but because someone is willing to vouch for you.

"Avoiding danger is no safer in the long run than outright exposure."

— Helen Keller

8 NICE GUY FINISHES LAST

A nice guy finishes last.

That lesson has followed me through much of my life, especially in moments where personal integrity collided with systems that rewarded compliance more than character. It is a difficult lesson, because it runs counter to the moral framework many of us are taught early on.

As a child, I was raised on a simple idea. Do good things and good things happen. Do bad things and bad things happen. It is a comforting belief, but adulthood teaches that life is rarely so orderly. Reality is often ambiguous, and outcomes are not distributed according to fairness.

I return to this lesson often when I think about my time in the military. I was deployed to Iraq as an Army Reservist during Operation Iraqi Freedom. At the time, I held the rank of E-4 Specialist and was actively preparing my promotion packet to Sergeant. On paper, I was doing everything expected of me. I had college credits, continuing education, and solid performance reviews.

The obstacle that repeatedly stopped my promotion was the Army Physical Fitness Test.

No matter what I did, I could not pass it consistently. I would improve one event only to fail another, usually by small margins, but enough to halt my progress every time. It became a cycle I could not seem to escape.

One day, between missions in Iraq, another soldier approached me and told me we were going to conduct a PT test so we could submit our promotion packets. I told him honestly that I did not believe I could pass a PT test under the conditions we were operating in. He reassured me and said not to worry. This test would be "best effort." Everyone would pass.

I declined immediately.

As much as I wanted a passing score and the opportunity to be promoted, I could not violate my own personal code. I told him I was not interested.

Later, two NCOs, noncommissioned officers, the enlisted leaders directly responsible for supervising soldiers and enforcing standards, approached me. They were responsible for organizing the test and wanted reassurance that I would not tell anyone about what was happening. What made the situation more complicated was that nothing was ever said outright. No one directly told me the test would be falsified. Everything existed in implication, rumor, and assumption, shaped by the pressures of deployment and mission tempo.

At the time, I was young and held a strong sense of moral certainty. I believed that what was being suggested was wrong. At the same time, context mattered. We were deployed in a combat zone, running fuel convoys. Team cohesion mattered. Trust mattered. A strong, functional team made those missions safer for everyone involved.

I made a choice.

I told the NCOs that I would not participate and would not assist in any way, but I would also not report the situation. As a lower enlisted soldier, I did not believe it was appropriate or necessary for me to intervene further. They could feel secure that I was not going to expose them.

The other soldier took the test and was promoted to Sergeant. He went on to have a successful military career.

Mine did not.

After deployment, my military career effectively ended. I left Iraq with lasting injuries, including PTSD and a traumatic brain injury. I completed my service obligation and accepted my discharge.

Even now, I find myself revisiting that moment. I wonder if I made a mistake. Had I taken that test, I likely would have earned my stripes. I had set two goals for my military career. I wanted to become a Sergeant, and after that, I wanted to be commissioned as a Second Lieutenant. I never aspired to high rank. I simply wanted to serve as an officer.

My father is a retired Navy officer, and I wanted to measure up. Not by following his exact path, but by standing on similar footing.

Yet when I ask myself what I would do differently if I could go back, my answer does not change.

Nothing.

I could not violate my own code. I needed to remain true to myself. And while the ethical line was not spoken aloud or formally crossed, I understood enough to know that participation would compromise something I was not willing to surrender.

Doing the right thing does not guarantee tangible rewards. It does not ensure success, promotion, or recognition. But it does allow you to live with yourself afterward.

And sometimes, that has to be enough.

"Only those who dare to fail greatly can ever achieve greatly."

— Robert F. Kennedy

9 SPLAT AWARD

For most of my life, I tried to avoid failure at almost any cost. Some of that came from untreated social anxiety. Some of it came from holding myself to internal extremely high standards that were not always realistic. I wanted to be good at things, ideally the best, and I did not want to tolerate failure even as a possibility. That mindset shaped a lot of my life. For example, I never dated much when I was younger because the fear of rejection felt overwhelming. Unfortunately, that same fear followed me into my professional life.

One story that captures this better than any other involves something called the SPLAT Award. I cannot even remember what the letters stood for anymore, but I remember the trophy clearly. It was a donkey, and it was given to the person who had most recently caused the largest outage. At the time, I was working in healthcare IT as a NOC technician, eager to prove myself and willing to take on anything I could get my hands on.

One day, a network architect asked me to clean up VLANs a type of network configuration, on some Cisco network gear. If you are familiar with Cisco commands, you know that removing VLANs requires precision. If you type the wrong command or press enter too quickly, you do not remove one VLAN, you remove all of them. That is exactly what I did. Unfortunately, I made that mistake on a piece of equipment that was critical to distributing network connectivity across the entire organization. In a matter of seconds, I effectively shut down network communication for an entire hospital.

In healthcare, outages are not just technical events. They affect clinicians, workflows, and ultimately patients.

The network engineer who had previously held the SPLAT Award was more than happy to pass it along. He set the donkey trophy on my desk. I was mortified. I felt ashamed, embarrassed, and deeply upset. I truly believed I had just proven myself to be a complete failure. I had taken down a hospital.

To be clear, I immediately contacted the network architect, explained what had happened, and owned the mistake. Working with local technicians, we rebooted the equipment, which flushed the configuration from memory and restored service. The technical issue was resolved relatively quickly. Emotionally, however, I was wrecked.

I remember walking into my manager's office, fighting back tears, and explaining how ashamed I felt. I told him how humiliating it was to receive an award for failure. I wasn't sure whether I was looking for reassurance or discipline. What I received instead was a lesson that has stayed with me ever since.

He looked at me and said, "Here's the deal. People who try to do great things have to take risks. And when you take risks, you will fail sometimes. The safest option is to do the bare minimum and minimize all risk. If you do that, you will not cause big outages like you did today. But you will also never be anything more than adequate."

What he gave me in that moment was psychological safety. He made it clear that accountability mattered, but learning mattered more. Years later, I would recognize this concept in the work of Amy Edmondson, who describes psychological safety as a shared belief that a team is safe for interpersonal risk taking. In that moment, my manager created space for learning rather than fear.

I could have learned to avoid risk entirely. Instead, I learned to manage it.

After thinking about it for a while, I decided to take control of the narrative around that failure. The donkey trophy was easy to find online, so I bought myself a copy. I had it custom engraved with "SPLAT Award" and the date I received it. Then I painted it gold and set it on my desk. I decided that if this failure was going to be part of my story, I was going to own it.

More importantly, I learned from it. One concrete change I made was to start using Cisco's "reload in X minutes" feature whenever I worked on critical network gear. That way, if I made a mistake, the system would automatically reboot and recover. There would still be an outage, and I would still have to explain it, but the risk was mitigated. I had turned failure into process improvement.

Over time, the SPLAT Award became something I was proud of. People would ask why I had a golden donkey on my desk, especially one that represented failure. My answer was simple. I was stronger because I failed. I understood the gravity of the work I was doing, the impact it had, and how to do it better.

That lesson carried over into other areas of my life, especially certification exams. Early in my IT career, I was trying to earn my Cisco CCNA. I failed that exam multiple times. Each failure felt crushing. At the time, it was the gatekeeper for my first real IT interview, and I had a young family to support. I had already realized that my biology degree alone was not going to provide the stability I needed without significant additional investment.

I kept taking the exam. I kept failing. And I kept learning. Each attempt showed me exactly what I did not understand well enough yet. I chose self-study instead of boot camps or shortcuts, and that meant the process was slower and more painful. But with each failure, I closed gaps in my understanding. Eventually, I passed.

Looking back, those failures were not setbacks. They were iterations. They were scaffolding. It was me building to a goal.

Later in my career, when others made mistakes under my watch, I remembered that moment in my manager's office and tried to respond the same way. Accountability still mattered, but fear was never the tool. Learning was.

I grew up believing that failure should be avoided, that it was something to be ashamed of. Over time, my experience has taught me the opposite. Failure, when driven by good intent and genuine effort, is not the obstacle to success. It is often the path to it. Failure only becomes an obstacle if you allow it to stop you.

The SPLAT Award sits in my memory as a turning point. It represents the moment I stopped fearing failure and started learning from it. In doing so, I became better at my work, more resilient as a professional, and more willing to take the kinds of risks that actually lead to growth.

"In any moment of decision, the best thing you can do is the right thing. The worst thing you can do is nothing."

— Theodore Roosevelt

10 BAD DECISION VS NO DECISION

Sometimes a bad decision, made quickly, is better than no decision at all.

After I returned from Iraq and settled back into school, I enrolled in ROTC, the Reserve Officers' Training Corps. On the surface, it looked like ambition. In reality, it was my way back into a military culture I had lost. While I was still a reservist, I lived military life every day for more than a year. After eighteen months deployed and then coming home to sleep in my childhood bedroom, I felt stalled. I needed a step forward. More than that, I wanted my community back.

I assumed I would stand out. I had been trained. I had deployed. I thought that experience would make me an all-star compared to most of my fellow cadets. Instead, I quickly realized I was not keeping pace. My peers were sharper, more practiced, and better adapted to the environment than I was. Whatever I had brought back with me from Iraq was not an advantage here.

That realization was difficult to accept. ROTC was supposed to confirm that I still belonged. Instead, it quietly suggested that the version of my military future I was holding onto no longer existed. My military career was already over. I just had not accepted it yet.

What I did not understand at the time was that I was also dealing with undiagnosed ADHD. One of the ways it showed up was through executive function paralysis, specifically the inability to initiate decisions.

I could weigh pros and cons endlessly. I could analyze every angle. I just could not move.

Executive paralysis is difficult to explain to people who do not experience it. Without medication, even simple tasks can feel impossible. Cleaning the house is a good example. I know it needs to be done. I make plans. I tell myself I will start in five minutes.

I don't.

The mess grows. What started as clutter becomes overwhelming. At some point, the task feels too large to begin at all. Before my ADHD diagnosis later in adulthood, I did not have language for this. I assumed the problem was a character flaw. I thought I was lazy.

To compensate, I relied on impulse. Sudden action was the only reliable way I could force movement. It worked often enough that I did not question the cost.

In one of my ROTC leadership courses, a captain said something that landed harder than he probably realized. On the battlefield, he said, you sometimes have to make a fast, bad decision, because no decision can be just as dangerous, if not worse. You rarely have complete information. Waiting for certainty can cost you everything.

That lesson explained a lot about my past.

Before I had language for what I was experiencing, the only way I could break out of paralysis was through decisive, often impulsive action. A clear example was my decision to enlist in the first place. I talked to every branch. The Air Force. The Marines. The Army. The Navy. I gathered information obsessively and still could not choose.

When I first talked to recruiters, I chased technical roles. IT. Technology. Something that felt aligned with who I thought I was. That door closed quickly. The Air Force was not interested based on my grades and my ASVAB results, which I had taken in high school mostly because it was a free test the school offered.

The Marines were never appealing. I spent weeks talking with a Navy recruiter. Submarines fascinated me from a technical standpoint, but I knew my fear of enclosed spaces would eventually become a structural problem.

The Army offered a similar job classification to the Marines, but I needed help with school more than I needed a perfect fit. So I did what I had done before. I found a new Army recruiter. I signed the paperwork. I was sworn in within a week.

I chose MOS 63J, Quartermaster and Chemical Equipment Repairer. It was a mechanic job, but not one that moved people from point A to point B. Smoke generators. Massive fuel pumps. Engines that existed only to support other systems. It was not glamorous, but it was decisive.

It was probably one of the best and worst decisions of my life.

The trajectory of my life would be unrecognizable without my deployment to Iraq and everything that came with it. I would not be the same person. At the same time, it was not an effective or healthy way to make decisions. It worked, but at a cost.

Impulse became my workaround for paralysis, but it did not always look impulsive at the time. Sometimes it looked reasonable.

While I was on my honeymoon during my first marriage, I ignored emails from the doctor who ran the research lab where I worked. My justification was simple. I was not in classes at the moment. It was a break. I told myself I would follow up when the next term resumed.

Part of what made that choice feel reasonable was that the lab was for college credit, not pay. Between academic terms, I was not receiving credit hours I had paid for, and there was no compensation involved. In my mind, that made the silence acceptable, even professional. I wasn't abandoning anything, I told myself. I was waiting for the system to resume.

When classes did resume, I scheduled a meeting with her. That was when I learned the decision had already been made. I would receive an Incomplete for the previous quarter. If I completed the lab work I had been assigned, the best possible outcome would be a C. I was no longer welcome in the lab, and I would not be part of the research team going forward.

Nothing explosive had happened. There was no argument. No confrontation. Just the quiet realization that by waiting, I had already chosen the outcome.

At the time, it felt like bad luck. Looking back, it was a familiar pattern. I delayed action until the window closed, then lived with the result as if it had been inevitable.

Some decisions are obvious. When I was a kid, we had a wooden bunk bed that started to collapse. It was about to fall onto one of my brothers. There was no analysis. You run. You stop the falling object. You protect the people you love.

Adult decisions are rarely that clean.

During my divorce, I tried to do what I had been taught was right. Be patient. Be passive. Trust that fairness would eventually surface. I believed restraint would be rewarded with justice.

It wasn't.

Passivity functioned as a decision, just not one that served me. I lost most of my physical property, including our family home. Waiting did not preserve anything. It simply allowed outcomes to solidify without my input.

I still struggle with decision-making. Sometimes I move too fast. Sometimes I wait far too long. I rely on consensus more than I probably should, leaning on family and friends to help me choose.

But that ROTC lesson stayed with me. I understand now that urgency changes the rules. If a car looks like it might merge into my lane on the expressway, I do not wait to confirm intent. I move first, then deal with secondary impacts. In moments like that, hesitation is not neutral. It carries its own risk, and sometimes the greatest danger comes from waiting too long to be certain.

I am still learning the difference between patience and paralysis. I do not always get it right. Sometimes I act too quickly. Sometimes I wait longer than I should. But I know now that refusing to decide is still a choice, and often the most expensive one.

"Forgiveness is giving up the hope that the past could have been any different."

— Oprah Winfrey

11 GRACE AND FORGIVENESS

Sometimes when people do bad things, grace is the right response. That is something I have had to learn throughout my life, and something I keep relearning. This is an important story to tell, even though I am nervous to tell it, because it is shameful and uncomfortable in a lot of ways.

As a child, I had an issue with stealing. I cannot tell you exactly why. It started small, food, treats, little things around the house, and over time it escalated to money. For the most part, this behavior stayed within the family. It was wrong, but contained.

I wanted things I did not have. But more than that, if I am being honest, I enjoyed the arms race between my parents and myself. Every new rule or safeguard felt like a puzzle. Every countermeasure invited a workaround. There was a rush in planning, scheming, and executing something successfully. For every limitation imposed on me, I could think of a way around it. I learned how to navigate constraints, how to exploit gaps, how to stay just ahead of consequences.

Afterward, I knew it was wrong. I felt guilty. But I learned how to push that guilt aside, how to rationalize my behavior, how to ignore the reality of what I had done. My parents noticed. They sent me to therapy, first for stealing and later for lying. Even now, as an adult, I cannot point to a single clear cause. I suspect there was some perceived need I did not know how to articulate, or did not feel was being met.

When I was around twelve, I became close friends with a classmate and spent a lot of time at his house. Over time, I noticed that his father kept petty cash in a desk drawer. And I stole from it.

Not because I needed the money. Not because I was desperate. There were simply things I wanted that cost money I did not have.

The night I was caught, it was very late, or very early. His parents had gone to sleep hours before. I remember listening carefully for every sound, pausing often, convinced that at any moment I would be discovered. I heard a noise I could not place. Panicking, I grabbed the cash and shut the drawer.

When I turned around, my friend was standing in the doorway.

I froze. I had nothing to say. No excuse. No explanation. He told me to pack my things and leave. I handed him the money and walked out, humiliated and ashamed.

I was terrified. And looking back, this is difficult to admit, but I was not terrified because I had betrayed a friend or violated his family's trust. I was terrified because I had learned something very early in life: when you steal and get caught, punishment follows. I was waiting for it.

I considered calling him the next day to beg him not to tell on me. I did not. Part of me knew I deserved whatever came next. I had very few friends, and I had just violated the trust of one of the most important ones I had.

For days, I was on edge. I waited for my parents to confront me. I waited for consequences. The reality I understood, even then, was that the punishment that would hurt the most was already in motion: the loss of one of my very few friendships.

But it never came.

A few days later, my friend called me. He told me I would be allowed back at his house, but that he would be watching me closely. I accepted immediately. I was grateful, but deeply uncomfortable. I did not believe I deserved that grace.

That forgiveness, and that lack of consequence, became one of the major pivot points of my life.

From that moment on, I made a conscious decision to try to be a better person. At first, I modeled myself after him. Even as a child, he was an extraordinarily selfless human being. His father was very ill, and part of my friend's daily responsibility was helping care for him, including deeply personal tasks no child should have to manage. He did it without complaint.

I decided I needed to be more selfless. I needed to think more about what other people needed and less about what I wanted.

That self-correction was real, and it mattered. I began to find joy in giving rather than receiving. Christmas became less about what I might get and more about what I could offer. But I may have overcorrected. I carried the shame of that moment with me far longer than necessary.

What I did not realize at the time was that recognizing grace and practicing it are not the same thing.

I understood what my friend had given me. I carried it with me. But for a long time, grace remained something I applied narrowly and selectively. It was personal, not universal. I knew how to appreciate forgiveness when I received it, but I was far less consistent about offering it broadly to others.

That did not fully change until much later, during a veterans' emotional intelligence course. Our cohort struggled. Tempers flared. People argued. Old habits, trauma, and pride surfaced in ways that threatened to fracture the group. At one point, the program leader paused the room and said something deceptively simple: we have to give each other grace and assume good intent until proven otherwise.

That idea landed differently than it ever had before.

It reframed grace as a discipline rather than a gift. Not something earned or bestowed selectively, but something practiced deliberately, especially when it was difficult. Especially when emotions were high. Especially when conflict made withdrawal or judgment feel justified.

That moment expanded grace for me from a personal lesson into a guiding principle. Not perfectly, and not universally. Even now, there are places where applying it remains hard. Coparenting with my ex-wife is one of them. I can understand grace intellectually while still struggling to live it emotionally in situations shaped by history, pain, and ongoing friction.

We did not speak directly about the incident again until years later, in college. It came out during a late-night, alcohol-fueled confession, the year before I deployed to Iraq. At the time, my drinking had increased, and I genuinely believed I might not come back. I told him everything.

He told me then, and many times since, that I had paid my debt. That I did not owe him anything.

I try to live as if that is true. But if I am honest, it still itches in the back of my mind. It was a childish decision, made by a child. But his grace is what helped me become the adult I am today.

I did not deserve forgiveness in that moment. But because I received it, I learned how to give it.

I am not advocating for people to be taken advantage of. I am not arguing against justice or accountability. But grace is an essential human quality, one that becomes rarer as we move into adulthood, into systems, into rules, into consequences.

And yet, without it, we lose something important.

Grace keeps us human.

"We don't change until the pain of staying the same is greater than the pain of change."

— Henry Cloud

12 GETTING HELP FOR THE WRONG REASON

Sometimes in life, you don't realize you need help until you're trying to help someone else.

My first marriage had a lot of problems. Some were rooted in the relationship itself. Others came from things I carried back with me from Iraq, including undiagnosed PTSD and issues I had not yet acknowledged, much less addressed.

At the time, I believed strongly in willpower. The idea of "pull yourself up by your bootstraps" was a constant theme in the military and in the stereotypical masculine culture I grew up in. Discipline solved problems. Endurance solved problems. If something was broken, you applied more effort.

After Iraq, I didn't want to admit that I was having problems. Instead, I decided that I could fix anything. My mental health, my physical health, even my marriage. All of it, I believed, could be handled with enough determination on my side.

That belief wasn't accidental. As I mentioned in an earlier chapter, my parents had sent me to therapy as a child for stealing and lying. At the time, my experience of therapy felt less like understanding and more like correction. It felt like adults telling me to obey, comply, and behave. I didn't walk away from those experiences feeling supported. I walked away believing therapy was about control, not insight. That belief stayed with me far longer than I realized.

When I returned from Iraq, I was not the same person. My deployment involved roadside bombs, occasional small-arms fire, and regular mortar attacks on our base. Even after returning home, I tried to seek treatment for PTSD. Like many soldiers from the Iraq War era, I was told I didn't qualify. I was told it was likely a preexisting issue.

That explanation never made sense to me.

Before Iraq, I loved fireworks. After Iraq, I could only tolerate them if I knew exactly where they were coming from and when to expect them. I knew something was broken. But I was being told the problem was internal, something inherent to me rather than something that happened to me. So I did what I knew how to do. I pushed forward and ignored it.

Emotionally, my world narrowed. I was angrier, more volatile, and far less regulated than before. I wouldn't describe myself as violent, but I reacted quickly and intensely. My ability to pause, reflect, or de-escalate was limited. Arguments with my ex-wife became frequent, and they often reached a point where my own feelings felt secondary to managing someone else's emotional response.

One argument escalated far beyond anything that should have happened.

I had just gotten out of the shower and was standing near my home office and kitchen when she grabbed a set of top-tier, extremely sharp kitchen knives and began throwing them at me. I believed I was in real danger. To stop it, I moved forward and tackled her to the ground so the knives would stop coming at me.

Afterward, I apologized. I also told her plainly that I believed my life had been in danger. She responded that this could be considered domestic abuse. I told her that if she believed that, she should call the police, though I didn't think it would go the way she expected.

The argument continued for a while. Eventually, I retreated to my computer and began researching therapy options. I found an online, self-guided program and suggested it. She rejected that idea. After more discussion, we agreed to resume marriage counseling in person.

Then I suggested that she might benefit from individual therapy.

She reflected that suggestion back at me and told me that I needed therapy for PTSD and anger. I agreed, not because I believed I had a problem that could be solved, but because I believed stability required it. I was willing to pay a procedural price if it meant the situation would improve. If that meant I had to be evaluated, I would do it, provided she did the same.

I didn't wait. I scheduled my appointment immediately and began treatment.

What followed surprised me.

At first, I didn't feel any different. In fact, it was other people who noticed the change before I did. They told me I seemed more together. That I didn't rage the way I used to. Over time, I began to feel it too. I still experienced the same emotions, but they arrived more slowly and with less force. There was space between feeling and reacting. Problems didn't disappear, but I could respond to them instead of exploding into them. Resolution became possible.

The improvement wasn't abstract or philosophical. It was practical and obvious.

My ex-wife did pursue some therapy, but it was sparse and surface-level, maybe once a month, and never very deep. Eventually, our marriage ended. I wish it hadn't. But there is only so much one person can do.

What did change was me.

Once I accepted help, it spread into other areas of my life I had neglected for years. I started seeing doctors. I went to the dentist. I saw an eye doctor. I stopped treating my own health as optional or secondary. As that happened, I also started exploring walls I had built for myself. I tried singing, something my ex-wife had mocked. I started running. Slowly. Very slowly. I completed several half marathons. I still haven't finished a full marathon, but I'm not done trying.

The original goal was to stabilize a failing relationship. That goal was lost. But somewhere along the way, I learned something more important.

Even if the initial reason was procedural, even if the insight came accidentally, I learned that I alone was worth the effort. I stopped treating myself as expendable in service of fixing something else. The marriage didn't survive, but I did. And that decision changed everything that came after.

"For every action, there is an equal and opposite criticism."

— Harrison Ford

13 THE COSTS OF CHANGE

Change always sounds exciting.

The reality is more complicated. Sometimes change is good. Sometimes it is painful. Most of us understand that instinctively. What we do not always stop to consider, and what I certainly did not consider carefully enough at the time, is how our personal changes ripple outward and affect the people around us.

When I applied to a veteran support group cohort, the program was highly selective and required a level of honesty I was not initially prepared to offer. I had to explain where I was in my life, how I had arrived there, and what I did not yet understand about myself.

I was rejected more than once.

Looking back, I understand why. My applications focused almost entirely on what I thought I could do with the program. I treated it like a gold star, something to earn and display. After mentoring from another veteran who had already completed the emotional intelligence course, I rewrote my application entirely. This time, I wrote about where I actually was, how my experiences had shaped me, and what I was struggling to understand rather than who I hoped to become next.

I had already made one of the most common mistakes people make with change. Instead of acknowledging where I was standing, I tried to leap directly to who I thought I could be.

There was another concern with that program that weighed heavily on me. Among married or partnered participants, the breakup and divorce rate hovered somewhere between twelve and twenty-five percent. That statistic scared me. The program explicitly allowed spouses to attend alongside participants, so I encouraged my spouse at the time to join me. My hope was that we could grow together, repair together, and emerge stronger as a couple.

She was not interested.

That pattern repeated itself elsewhere in my life.

For years after leaving the military, I struggled with my weight. At my heaviest, I was approaching three hundred and fifty pounds. I tried to solve the problem the way I had been taught to solve everything else in life: willpower. Diet harder. Run more. Push through. None of it worked in a lasting way.

What many people do not realize is how hard bariatric surgery is even before the operation. Insurance requirements demanded months of documented dieting, weigh-ins, and weight loss targets. I remember surviving on tiny portions, often just small pieces of cheese when hunger hit. After the surgery, recovery was brutal. I had never experienced surgical pain before, and suddenly my body felt foreign to me.

I also had to give myself daily injections to prevent blood clots. Despite years of trying to overcome a fear of needles, including tattoos, that phobia never fully disappeared. Giving myself injections was one of the most difficult parts of the entire process.

Ironically, my then wife was the one who first suggested bariatric surgery, years before I seriously considered it. What eventually made the option feel real was discovering that, through my job in healthcare, I qualified for a substantial employee discount. The surgery shifted from something monumental and unreachable to something expensive, but attainable.

Still, I resisted.

Part of that resistance was deeply tied to how my military career had ended. Bariatric surgery is disqualifying for military service. It would effectively close the door on any future attempt to reframe or redeem that chapter of my life through reentry or commissioning. That policy is not punitive; it reflects the logistical reality that the military is built around uniformity, including nutritional needs. Still, knowing that the door would close permanently made the decision feel heavier.

At the same time, I was forced to confront another truth. Obesity was not a cosmetic issue. Left unaddressed, it could easily take ten or twenty years off my life.

What ultimately pushed me forward was not self-love, at least not in the way people like to imagine it. It was responsibility. I had children. They needed me healthy and present for as long as possible. And, candidly, the affordability of the surgery mattered. I did not need to save for years or hope for some mythical job bonus. It was possible now.

There was significant friction afterward. My now ex-wife was not pleased with the changes. The dynamic of our relationship shifted in ways that felt asymmetrical, as if my growth highlighted a distance neither of us knew how to bridge. This is speculation on my part, but I believe some of that tension stemmed from her own dissatisfaction with her body and the belief that I had taken a shortcut toward becoming closer to the version of myself I envisioned.

In hindsight, one of my biggest blind spots was failing to fully consider how these changes would affect the people around me. Bariatric surgery is deeply personal, but it still alters family dynamics, self-perception, and how others see you. I am profoundly glad I made the choice, but it required crossing a line.

I had to give up optionality.

The same truth about change and its secondary impacts is true in leadership decisions as well. Leadership decisions will ripple outward regardless of intent. Some of those secondary effects will be positive, some neutral, and some negative. Pretending otherwise does not prevent the consequences; it only delays our reckoning with them.

I had to close doors in order to do what was best for me. At the time, I justified the decision through practicality and responsibility. Today, I would like to believe I would make it simply because I am worth it. But back then, it was enough to know that my family needed me, and that this was the path that allowed me to stay.

Sometimes change demands that we choose ourselves, even when doing so reshapes everything around us.

"You are allowed to be both a masterpiece and a work in progress."

— Sophia Bush

14 CLOSING

I wrote this book at a moment when forward progress stopped feeling obvious.

In my case, being stalled did not look like failure from the outside. It looked like maintenance. I went to work, fixed problems, and stayed carefully within a highly defined lane. The work mattered, but mostly when something broke. When things were working, I was largely invisible. Positive attention felt distant. Innovation existed, but mostly as maintenance. Within my team, I had the freedom to improve how we worked and how we solved problems. What I did not have was a path to influence how the larger organization operated. Meaningful change felt bounded by role rather than effort. Over time, that boundary began to feel less like structure and more like inertia.

Safety plays a convincing role in that kind of environment. For a long time, it seemed like the responsible choice. And in truth, I could likely put significantly less effort into my work and even my personal life and maintain the status quo. It would be boring, but stable. Predictable. The longer I sat with that reality, the more I realized something uncomfortable. Safe work is not neutral. It is a choice. Hard work and innovation carry the risk of visible failure. Safe work quietly accepts a different kind of failure, one that is smaller, less obvious, and easier to justify. Over time, that kind of failure accumulates.

I explored several paths while trying to understand what to do with that realization. The Doctor of Information Technology program sharpened my thinking and improved my performance at work, but it also created friction. I wanted to do more, see more, and contribute differently. That desire did not always align with the role I occupy today. Art forced a different lesson. I carried an idea in my head for years and avoided it out of fear. When I finally tried it, it failed. It was not the glowing mesh of wood, resin, and light I had imagined, but something disappointing and incomplete. That failure pushed me to rethink the design and, in the process, rediscover older, more familiar ways of creating. Writing has been its own experiment. Academic writing taught structure and discipline. Writing this book reminded me that exploration can still be enjoyable, even when clarity is incomplete.

What you have read is not a set of instructions or a formula for success. These stories are moments where leadership, growth, and failure unfolded in real time. Often imperfectly. Often without confidence. Rarely according to plan.

My understanding of leadership has changed over time. As a child, leadership looked fearless, selfless, and decisive. It looked like certainty. Now it looks more like service. It looks like honesty delivered with care. It looks like emotional intelligence, self-awareness, and the willingness to say difficult things without losing empathy. That shift did not come from theory. It came from experience, friction, and mistakes.

This book is for people who believe they did everything right and still failed. Sometimes failure is unavoidable. Sometimes it is learning in disguise. Sometimes it is both at the same time, and the distinction only becomes clear much later.

This book may have been useful to you. It may not have been. Either outcome is acceptable.

One of the harder lessons I have learned is that persistence alone is not always the answer. When something is not working, pushing harder can deepen the problem rather than solve it. Growth sometimes requires a pivot. A step away from what feels safe. A willingness to try something unfamiliar without guarantees.

I do not know exactly where this path leads next. I only know that relying exclusively on what worked before was no longer enough. Writing this book did not resolve that tension. It simply marked a moment where I chose to acknowledge it.

ABOUT THE AUTHOR

Matthew West-James is a professional in information technology, a veteran of the United States Army, and a lifetime learner who has developed his career path through the intersection of technology, leadership, and human systems. His background has included network management, disaster recovery efforts, enterprise network infrastructure, and operational readiness in a manner that has consistently emphasized people and processes over technology and tools.

As a veteran of the United States Army, with experience in Iraq, Mr. West-James's early understanding of leadership was developed in environments where the outcomes of decision-making were of great consequence. These early influences have stuck with him through a decidedly unconventional career path that has been marked by success, stasis, transformation, and a series of tough turns. Along the way, he has come to recognize that many of the approaches that were thought to be drivers of success have, in actuality, become barriers to it.

He holds a Bachelor of Science in Biology and a Master of Science in Managing Information Technology, is currently pursuing a doctorate, and works in healthcare information technology. As a man of multiple passions, he is also a husband, father, volunteer, and practicing artist in media such as writing and mixed media. He aligns with the notion that development is rarely linear, leadership is often an undoing, and that unlearning is sometimes as valuable as learning.

www.ingramcontent.com/pod-product-compliance
Lightning Source LLC
Chambersburg PA
CBHW031210090426
42736CB00009B/861